DATE DUE

JUL 0 2 2008		
SEP 2 2 2008		
JAN 1 2 2011		
MAR 2 8 2011		
GAYLORD		PRINTED IN U.S.A.

F
B

2007

Cover image by   Renée van der Stelt

Author photo by   Author

Published in the United States by   Fence Books
                                        303 East Eighth Street, #B1
                                        New York, NY 10009
                                        www.fencebooks.com

Book design by   Rebecca Wolff

Fence Books are distributed by   University Press of New England
                                        www.upne.com

and printed in Canada by   Westcan Printing Group
                                        www.westcanpg.com

Library of Congress Cataloguing in Publication Data
Celona, Tina Brown [1974-]
Snip Snip!/Tina Brown Celona

Library of Congress Control Number: 2006938243

ISBN 0-9771064-5-4

FIRST EDITION

Grateful acknowledgment is made to the editors of the following
magazines, in which some of these poems first appeared: *Shampoo, Octopus
Magazine, La Petite Zine, Radical Society, Puppyflowers, Born Magazine, Monsieur
Toussaint Louverture, can we have our ball back?, Double Room.*

Tina Brown Celona

SNIP SNIP!

SNIP SNIP!

FOR YOU

TABLE OF CONTENTS

THE SEWING BOX

I wonder when I'll write a poem again
It would be so exciting
Writing it and then reading it after
Sometimes when you want to write poetry the most
You can't write it, and
Then you have to go out and get drunk.
A co-worker told me once
She thought poets led virtuous lives
I was sorry to disillusion her,
I don't think she believed me
I remember when I had opinions
It's not good to marry too young
You haven't known enough people
Wow those love poems were really good
I wish I could write a great love poem
Most men are not emotional like women
perhaps that's why there are very few poets
who write with feeling
the women imitating the men
the men thinking too much
I definitely have entertainment issues
I like to make people laugh

Poets in general are a vain lot
You can always come on to them
By admiring their poems
Falling in love with a poet is very exciting
When they are complicated that is exciting
And when they are moody
That is also exciting
Other men don't have that
Star quality

I feel terrific today
I live on your love
And don't need to eat.
How about some yogurt?
Mmm, that sounds good.
People who don't eat dairy are crazy
How's that for an opinion
No wonder people find me infuriating
But it's better than being ignored!
We do have our opinions
About most things
But that doesn't mean our opinions
Are better than other people's   Snip snip
Is what I do to my poems.
I'm going to call my book
Snip snip! What do you think?

POP CORPSE

When I'm older I write only once a week. The rest of the time I heal and drink juice cocktails and read and talk to people. This method seems to work for me and over time I even start to fart poems. The Corcoran asks me to do an exhibit of poems associated with infrared photographs of farts.

A boy can be your boyfriend without actually being your boyfriend. On the way you stop to wander through Glen Echo Park. The ancient cries of fun echo and re-echo. Years later I remember holding your hand. My memory is unreliable.

Favorable notice in another paper. On the fire escape the man asked me if I had hyperthyroid condition. Offended, I insisted that my thyroid was normal.

I realize that I have been as repressed in my poetry as I have been foolish in real life. When my writing goes well I attribute it to God. When I kissed you in the car I blamed myself. We were in the church for hours discussing our favorite cathedrals. There is always something I have not bothered to remember.

You are my secret best friend. I am a gas station attendant. When someone gives me a tip it is like I have done something great. I feel great as I pump gas.

UNTITLED (AFTER CERAVOLO)

All day
At his desk. Pink nectar
Floats on it.

Fly, bumblebee, fly.
You take my heart away.

The best one can do is Florida.
From Carolina,
Caroline.

Fly, bumblebee, fly.
You take my heart away.

What is the name for
            emotion? careless,
left out.

The hysteria is pink.
Sticky tongues
grow on it.

Fern-white temples.
O fish,
am I the bumblebee
in the sun's cause?

SUNDAY MORNING CUNT POEM

I wrote a book of contiguous poems then mixed them up so they were out of order. They were poems about my cunt, language, Nature, war, and all of them were marked with drama.

With the cunt poems I could have orgasms during sex. I had long, luxurious hair, which I wrapped around my throat like a scarf. You could say I was "released from my prison." My therapist was no longer busy.

We started a business called Ethical Donuts. It was actually a kind of juice bar where you could go and read poems or listen to someone reading poems. If nobody felt like reading poems we would turn on a tape of someone reading poems, usually one of our friends, but sometimes a big star of poetry. Of course, we sold donuts.

In my dream we were hitchhiking to Iowa City, but later when I looked at myself my cheeks were pink and so were my labia. Like a bird I discovered I had wings. I flew higher and higher, but when I got near the sun the wax melted and I fell into a poem by Auden. It was then that I wrote the poem "The Enormous Cock."

For a while I hushed. Then I started up again about my cunt. Some said it was a vicious swipe at feminism. Others said it was a vicious feminist swipe. It was the only word I knew.

VARIATIONS

There is some rotting fruit on the ground, a melon and some bananas. The men are sated and lie back on the ground naked. They are interested in each other's athleticism and their interest is not sexual. Where are the women? The women are absent. The colors are green and gold and black (shadow). I want to fight the men who look so tired. I want to revive them and straighten their shoulders. I want to transpose them to another painting and wipe their faces and give them sustenance. I want to give them milk.

+++

The woman has a man's face. She is staring at her parts. Her breasts denote womanhood. She is in gray. She is naked and she props herself up on her arms. The ground takes up most of the canvas. I want to fight her and hide her belly folds. I want to fight myself with all my arms against all my arms. The pain causes me to become rigid and when I fight myself I know I am not coming back. This is totally fine with me.

THE GREY PENGUIN POEMS

1.

The grey penguin
Looks for his wife.
He is alone on the ice
And he is lonely for his wife.

He is lonely
for his wife
so he dives.

A leopard seal tries to eat him
But the grey penguin
Is too fast.
He knows he must survive
To rejoin his wife.

So he sits on the ice.

2.

The grey penguin
Is in my hair. The grey penguin
Is in my wife's hair.

The grey penguin
Is a blonde.

I fought with myself
To close my eyes.

Szzz! said the lightning.

I give you thirty seconds
To locate
The grey penguin.

BOOK THROW UP

My poem was like a crash of cymbals
Ugly noises smashed together.
My eyes bulged.
That's all I wanted—for them to bulge.

I hate the thought of birthing a book.

Book throw up.

I THREW AWAY MY GUN AND MY HARNESS

I threw away my gun and my harness. I was no longer a superhero. Imagine this most ideal of situations: one's eye is forever lighting on beautiful things, one's emotions are aroused, one's hand expresses these emotions through the pen, which sentiments are interpreted by another, causing (in this scenario) the other to feel and see. Imagine this glorious image blotted out by a sinister black cloud. Imagine the cloud leaking and the drops spattering and diving among the flowers. When will men stop desiring young girls? He goes to work early wearing his most handsome shirt.

For an hour I take pictures of my cunt. Spread cunt, panties pulled askew, prim virginal cunt, cunt with asshole, cunt without asshole. I make a photo album, one cunt on each page.

I never wrote the ending of this poem. You are not reading it now.

POEM FOR GIRLS

1.

You can read all about yourself in this poem
And that's why it's fun.
Everyone wants to be in this poem
But this poem is only for girls.

2.

In spring the barberry leaves are lettuce-red.
In fall they are the color of the sun
As it explodes.
The willows leaf out
Long before the oaks.
You're thinking about your computer as a girl
And I'm jealous.
I think, "It doesn't make me want to quote it,"
And then I think "happy disco-colored elephants."

3.

There is always a more
Truthful truth. Sensitive, beautiful emotions
Swirl around me like snowflakes.
I look at the cat.
One of us has farted.

HAND WITH JAR

There was a hand. There was a jar, the hand was lifting the lid off the jar and nearby there was a big red fruit. To the left and in the distance were ferns. To the bottom center and right the sun was coming up. A blue Egyptian flower sprouted from the branch on which the red fruit was growing. It looked like the jar was standing on a table. The important thing was the circle of light around the jar. You could not look away from it, you could not look at the painting without looking at the jar, because the painting was so small that all of it could not fill up your whole eye.

The three objects were evolving. One was a collection of safety pins. One was a tropical fruit. The three were like weapons with sharp, knifelike edges and you could not tell if they were the same size on either side.

I was certain you were a genius. Your paintings were the size of your ego. Your notebooks were a place to hide them.

HOLA, COWBOY!

I am invited to a baby shower. It takes a while to sink in. On the phone she thought she sounded oddly formal. She was trying to remember what came next in this particular "interaction with another person." Why should she have been invited?

That day I tried to trick myself out of writing by vacuuming and dusting between poems. In those few weeks after the rain there was nothing but bumblebees obscenely penetrating the foxgloves—the regular bees had all died. Then, one day, as I was staring absently out the window, I saw one small bee fertilizing a clover flower, like a mailman delivering sperm.

EVENT DIARY

That evening I am thrilled to discover I am still alive. I breathe and it makes a whistling sound. I gnash my teeth and make Dracula faces and stay outside in the car until it is too late.

When I finally do it I realize I have been putting it off all day. The polar bear tipped me off but I was still surprised when I woke up this morning with a rubber heart.

The elements of our day were as follows: church, graveyard, community garden, Luna Park, museum park, museum, car, Golden Gate Park, bar, reading, car. I reach for my coffee nastily as a dumbbell nebula fizzes in the distance.

Is there any more?

Naturally there is, there's John Godfrey. He's come all the way from Brooklyn and Bill Berkson, Leslie Scalapino, and Kevin Killian are in the audience. Bill and Kevin ignore me but Leslie says hi.

There's a field full of nasturtiums and a ratty columbine and the headlight crashes down the trash chute to land in a quivering pile of filaments and Tic Tacs. I light a little pyre in the yard and wander around aimlessly thinking about things. Then I realize the things are actually thinking about me.

QUARREL

The man and his wife quarreled.
Their cat's ears smelled like a doughnut.
No, said the man, they smell like muffins.
No, said the wife, they smell like pannetone.
I'll have mine with coffee, decided the husband.

The wife set off in the wrong direction.
The husband added that it was "patently untrue."
What is there to be sad about, asked the man of his wife.
The wife blubbered some more.
The man crossed her out and shut his notebook with a bang.

METAPHORS

She is hiding the poem under the bed. It is dark under the bed and it smells like cat. It is raining out. Fortunately for poetry it is raining.

My heart is a box lined with tears. They sparkle like diamonds. They sparkle for you.

He is in Nice attending a conference. The astronomers are acting like monkeys. They hotly debate the Anthropic Principle while holding on by their tails. They are learned and fearful and they joke as they twist their tails and beam.

There is a string of bees in the box.

She reads about Paul Klee in the hope that it will interest him but she herself is not interested and so she desists after 1902. In 1902 Paul Klee became more interested in God than in his wife.

I write words on the forehead and around the corners of the mouth. My human faces are truer than real ones.

There is a glow-in-the-dark owl in the box.

You are sleeping. Dreams glide through your brain: stars collapsing, universes expanding, numbers assembling. I dream of losing a pair of red shoes.

NERUDA SUITE

MY ENEMY-FRIEND

The wine is worming my enemy-friend.
This treats of a man encumbered
In his green, in his cigar
Like a case of hither
Whose next breath
Has the singular swordfish
Who loves me with vertigo.

Miring the years in their roster
In his eyes tepid water
In the lines of the sun
Submit one's own
Slowly, reserved and prideful.

Let's dress in the clearing
Of shivering weeds
In the wind that parches the ground
And fights with the sky.
A man's dog, alone and wearing
New leaves, the road
Of all doors. I believe
That behind the ibis the silence
That no one understands
Takes a stone to the hymn:
It will last the duration.

ZOO

The clandestine antelope
Undresses in the fog
Her hiccups nourished on
The similar collar of humans.

Of the ornamented horn
With the animal tied to his master
Resolving an extraordinary system
Of ardent foodstuffs
Descending like punctuation
And a compassionate amber collar.

WATER

The roasted wind
Multiplies against the light
That is the flower of juvenile eyes
Embedded in the world.

I desert the dry rocks.

Under these circumstances
I flex my neck:
Eternity in eternal water.

WHEN I TAKE OFF MY TOP HAT

When I take off my top hat
I tap my head:
Despite the suave fugue
As if wine and egg
Separated.
A newborn ant, claret
Across my foot
Boosted the circulation, wiped its antennae
Ascending a rapid stairway
The slow vulva that you are:
Meat and foot: entire enemies.

THE LICHEN AND THE STONE

The lichen riding on the stone
Gummy and green, encircling
The blue mass of the jerboa,
Extends its writing
On the sea
Of rented rocks.
The lee of the earth, the murderous mollusks
And the reverted fish
Skip from stone to stone.
In the long and significant silence
You can hear the clear caddy of the coast.

The liquor I extend to my mother
Comes and goes like boobs:
Folded in the grunting air.
It seems we are bathing in water
That neither comes nor goes.

DYING

How to remove one from oneself
The disconnected rattle
Abrogating the testicles of cows,
Depositing the movement
Of the free air, the green wind.
Where no one declines
Unless there is a shady election,
A rising elevator
Of the dead eyes' retreat?

The official algae
Is establishing a raise
That will never be established,
Because the curiosity
Ravages the heart
Even as the virus ravages the lips and mouth.
Look at the pies
The friends will assent to.

RAZOR

The oblong razor
Seemed not to move
As if the daylight
On its forehead
Inclined it to describe
The puddles on the floor
The moon singing bitterly
In the night of eels.

GOLF

When you drag me
To the golf course
You must guard against
My razor and my sister's razor
Like the large cockroach seen
asleep in his carapace
Discussing our destruction.

Tales are very hairless —
A volcano in a cup
Tends your spirit, arranges yours
On the only, melancholy page.
With a green sun star
Snuffling there
As it describes my entire life,
Without words or interpretation:
A solitary shadowed gulf
In pale arms.

CATCH-FLOWER

The seven petals of the sea
Joined with the sun's corolla
In a loving diadem:
A red buoy
Leaps enamored
Of the thousand lips of the ovary
Of a rose so delicious
It lisps both sun and salt.

DINKY LOGIC

I was ill from the mental rays. They shot them with their eyes. People who matter never notice when you compliment them on their glasses. Or on their parrot.

I moved to a safer place away from the mental rays. I bent my eyes down. They did not want me to help with their party.

As the mountain lion explained, he did not get along with the other mountain lions. He would get along with the ewes because they liked the shape of his groin. But he was not a favorite among the mountain lions.

MARMALADE

There are a lot of things you can say in poetry
That won't go in conversation.
Nobody would look at me
So I ate two pieces of pie followed by a potato.
Later you asked me if anyone
Had been mean to me. No, I replied,
Scuffing my heel in the dirt.
The following morning we were in the orchard.
I nearly touched the sunburn on your arm
Remembering the onion marmalade.

APHTHOUS ULCER

I have an aphthous ulcer
On my throat. It is the size of a grape,
But flat.

I have an aphthous ulcer
The color and pattern of my favorite socks.
Smoke scars my throat.

I can no longer finish
My aphthous ulcer pie.
It sings in a mysterious voice.

I rejected the aphthous ulcer
And with glacial scorn
Relaxed my frown.

TRIXIE NAILS NED, AND

Nancy is pissed.
She throws a bomb in the igloo
And the igloo explodes and there's snow everywhere.
The grey penguin waddles over
To his devoted wife, who's
Cowering in a corner.
He grasps her firmly by the beak
And leads her into the
Snowy antechamber.

STANZAS IN MEDITATION

The poem is like a farm
You finish before five.
The chickens are like commas.
There's nothing sacred
About our blue tractor.
People like metaphors
So we implant them. Your eye is
A tiny hole. A gift of meat.

The farm is like a poem
Torturing us for fun.
The apples are oysters
Cracking open the trees.
They've done nothing wrong
Except shelter bees.
Hard work is a selfish dream.
That's what the bees hum.

SNACK

When you wake up
You will have a snack. How can you let
Them see what you
Think you look like?
What you think it is
OK to look like?

ISSUES OF GENIUS

She is competing in a race in which one runs across water in flippers, and sidestrokes with someone else holding on. She is the slowest. Afterwards one tries to buy supper but can only afford U-need-a Biscuits.

She is reading the *Autobiography of Alice B. Toklas* and learning about genius.

Every morning she gets up to see her husband off, then goes back to bed. She wakes up around lunchtime and eats. Then goes back to bed until dinner. Then goes back to bed.

Her friend writes to tell her that Nietszche said genius is a fiction forged by those who put it on a pedestal so they don't have to measure themselves with it, and that she (her friend) has decided she does not believe in genius, nor is interested in the question of genius, that she has decided this recently, if not life would be unlivable.

Gertrude Stein has a thing for genius. She has met three geniuses in her lifetime: Alfred Whitehead, Pablo Picasso, and herself. That is pretty few!

SPRING IN PARIS

The wind in my bikini
is not in my bikini after all.
It lurks in the strings
And in the soft flap
Between my legs,
and it is waving like a flag
on the raft of the Medusa
in the Louvre in Paris
or wherever the Louvre may be now.

By the fur of Maurice the dog I love you.

I admit the sand of the rooftop, the fish of the friary,
the eggs of the amoeba, the beak of the apothecary.

By the last drop of wine
in the smallest glass I beseech you

By the yellow fuzz
on the banana slug

I entreat you.

How can I tell him that everything
is useless without you
to hear, you
with your cultivated ear.

DISCOURSE (AFTER PAUL KLEE)

The picture of the monster getting ready to eat another monster is my favorite. Don't ask me what a yin-yang is doing between them, or why they seem to be emerging from the shadows. They both have their mouths open as if they are breathing or screaming.

Here is an animal biting a man. It is on his back and it is biting him from behind. They look like a maze.

Here he is preaching to the animals in the desert. They are shrimp-creatures. If it were in color his heart would be pink. He is happy to see them. He is raising his crook to them.

I like *The Book Of Ancient American Proverbs* but I *love* you.

A horse is standing up on its hind legs. Another horse is pawing the ground. It is the Scene of Comical Riders. In all there are three horse-beasts and one rider.

I want to ask Renée what she thinks of Paul Klee but I am too embarrassed. I am glad Renée does not ask me what I think of X.

A cloud is following that train. Or perhaps a giant elbow.

I am not yet at the point where I breathe poetry. Can I end the poem like this? In this picture her head is broken off and his arm is cheese.

Robin is bringing me lotion. I love her—I love Robin. She is a talented aromatherapist. She and Amy and Frank—they are all good people. The interesting thing about Dr. Friedes is he does not eat vegetables. He is a steak and hamburger man. That's OK—my family is carnivorous too.

FOURTH OF JULY

The J from the Scrabble set is next to my typewriter. I crush my
thighs and examine the cellulite. I always wanted to be pretty, and now
I'm thirty. Last summer I said, My days of wearing a bikini are over.
And if I can't wear a bikini, I don't want to go swimming.

This morning we walked about a mile out over the tide flats avoiding,
as you called it, crab habitat. It was a long day that began with
donuts and ended with explosions over the river. On our way in to
Provincetown my shoelace got caught in the gears of my bike and
I did a slow controlled fall into some mulch. I wonder how long I'll
remember that it was brown. So much mulch is red these days.

My doctor tells me I'm hostile and I disagree. I don't need another
cigarette but I smoke one on the stairs because the poem is going well.
You wake up and come to the door and gaze at me sorrowfully. Why
aren't you sleeping? I ask you. I might as well ask you, why don't you
mind your own business? The moon shines like a piece of candy.

I ought to thank you for taking me home. Another day might have
been the end of me—I found myself hunting for a rope and a closet.
While you were swimming I sat on the porch and gazed at a pine
tree and thought unavailingly of someone to write to. Then I called
everyone I could think of.

Something unusual always happens when you least expect it. If I
hadn't agreed to come along with you to the batting cages I might not
have learned what I did, if you know what I mean. I realize I'm being
very mysterious but you never can tell who reads poetry these days.

My doctor says I'm hostile and I believe him. He says I've been hostile from the start and I tell him I'm just testing him. I smoke another cigarette to dispel the taste of rum. Rum—intoxicant—bad. Cigarettes—bad. Poetry, too, is bad for you.

I think of my job at the school and how much I hated it and I vow never to work again. You don't know what I've been writing in these cover letters. A writer is the worst kind of parasite. God knows what Janice is telling them—Janice who thinks Camrys are boring.

MOUSES OF MISERY

I danced like an elf on top of a mushroom.
The mushroom bent under my ponderous steps.
I straddled the mushroom and invoked the Creator.
This met with no reaction and I considered
Pontificating about widowhood.

I danced like a midget on the corpse of my benefactor.
It collapsed, consumed by voracious euphemisms.
With a roll of the die I summoned the Deity.
With a loll of the head you inflicted the TV.
I knew then that wisdom was not a brand of beer.

The elves of my mushroom rotated like
Dirty sheep in their hive.
It burned, sending up tumors of honey.
Flotillas of dolphins floated me to freedom.
Mouses of misery chastened me in my solitude.

I mushed on my mushroom to nodules
Of nonsense. The cavernous chateau
Wet me like the Nile. Holy, holy
Chanted the nurses of Creation.
A thousand nuts spilled from their wimples.

ODE TO A BEAUTIFUL NUDE

Your heart is cast in the pure eye of time.
I celebrate you, lover of bosky air
Aromatic with earth, humming and marine.
Lovely nude, your feet arc in a satin gulp
To the faltering sea, your life
Cast like flowering velvet on its waters,
Dividing into pallid regions of surging stones,
Turgid fruits of fine alabaster.
Your body, material and symmetrical,
Twists, mortal, aggregate
Of memory and flat unpetaled pulchritude.
I have exchanged your feminine nose
For a puddle winking at the moon.

AT THE RATE OF TWO POMPOMS A DAY

At the rate of two pompoms a day
You recorded your impressions of death.
I was easier with myself and when I drank wine I was easier still.
The silence on Sunday was deafening, as was the seepage
In the closet under the stairs.
Traveling burned off my cleverness.
The contents of my brain were insipid and tasteless.
I washed off the broom with detergent, then set it back in the closet.
It was hard to write about asparagus in pea season;
Death glared like an inconstant toad.
My friend stepped off the plane and into my life.
Her distraction was beautiful.
"Why don't you wear that hat with the shades?"
To this she responded with a long, shallow moan.
"You wear your nonsense like a pompom."

MAN WITH GUN

He writes a letter because he can't write a poem.
He is afraid he will never be known for anything but his letters.
He teases the languid mushroom with his nose, then flips it to his doe.
He discovers his ethnicity.
The planes roar overhead, rattling the windows.
He goes to walk the dog but there is only the leash.
He cooks his meal in the dark and eats it without looking.
He sleeps like a child with a beard.
He paints a nude without a live model.
He wipes his nose on his sweatpants.
Later he devours a lobster, sucking noisily on its legs.
His prison is more like a desert island.
He pulls the fibrous husks of coconuts to pieces and lights fires in
the sand.
He dreams that everyone hates him and that this is because of his art.
He dreams that his sister throws a beach umbrella at his head, and that
he laughs it off, then realizes he ought to have reprimanded her.
He scrutinizes the bruises on his knees. They remind him of the clouds
on the moon.
He interviews for another job, it is May and he loosens his tie, unlaces
his shoes and lies in the grass chewing thoughtfully on a stem.
He is called back for a second interview.
Just as he expects, it does not go well, so he fires his water pistol in
agony—once, twice, three times.

EGO SALAD

I made my ego salad with organic mayonnaise. I added onions and a touch of pepper. Would you like to have some? Some people hold you have to cook the ego in cold water and let it sit. I find it easier to peel my ego when it's warm.

Everyone I fed my ego salad to had a stomachache except you. You ate it gladly and you even asked for more. In Oswego they eat ego salad all the time—it's even more popular than clam strips in Revere.

You can't have ego salad without personal toast. Personal toast comes in five flavors: Mine, Yours, Theirs, Ours, and Hers.

HUNGARIAN CAFÉ

I know a Hungarian café
I will take you to
This will be a present to you
Dearest who are not expecting it
Who says sadly
"No one likes us" "what have we done"
At night finding someone has left
A fork in the potted plant

POEM ABOUT NOTHING

I wrote the poem about nothing on a blue day with squibs in the sky.
I built it like a house I had read about in a book.
I furnished it with cleverness and technical sofas.
Visitors came to the house and endowed it with taffeta.
Evidence of previous visitors showed in the absence of tulle.
I wondered if the moon would ever hang around the rafters and fill the
straw of my bed with alpine flowers.
You were sensitive to the slightest gurgle; you flinched at the tiniest
palpitation.
The poem about nothing receded glittering.
Upon first sight of you I felt rapture, and then a dead calm.
What I wanted to do was slow and transformative.
You yelped something indefinite about escape.

POEM

I can see way down.
I can see pretty far away.
I can gauge the speed of a moving vehicle.
I can tell the truth
Or I can tell a lie.
I can see your face
Approaching across the yard.
I press my eyes
Into my head
With my knees.

. . .

HIGHLIGHTS FROM THE PERMANENT COLLECTION

The point luminates like a tiny candle.
Just like the virgins, I lactate sympathetically.

+++

I have a trajectory. I am a paper airplane.

No eighties rock star
                    I
                        Heave through it —
Like snowy white bread crumbs on a winter night.

Stop me, I am peeling the brain
Of my paper airplane.

red trinket

flung enthusiastically into the fray

+++

It is likelier to last if it is longer
though it is more likely that your aunt, a strict Catholic, will be horrified

the book with the dreadful cover is best
though I don't like the cover

First thought, ordinary thought

> Several stars shine
> like luminescent badgers.

Pause the mule, I say. As usual my poems are full of monsters but like
Paul Klee I decorate them with flowers. I need to shift to the right just
a little to be able to see over the man in front of me.

and lo, it happened that there was meat and fish and fowl and eggplant
at the wedding . . .

I grabbed one of my balloon tow-ropes . . .

He is an urban cowboy. He is from Brooklyn. That is what I love
about him.

+++

I want to discipline myself but I am already gone. I am gone until I go
to sleep. Then I am home. The star on my nightstand flickers. On the
sled of my poem I coast into your life.

Knowing there is more where that came from

As we kissed behind a pillar of the church.

Pain and anger vied for control as I stamped my feet and huffed
through my nostrils.

It's time to reach for that book again

you thought
was boring

and I couldn't stop writing about it. The fairy wren
hops on the rotting vegetables. I disappear tomorrow
but while you are in the bathroom
our crumbs are cleared away. Naturally I go back

and peer through the Viewmaster.

+++

sullenly spitting out poems
the independent wife
censored her cunt poems
as if life
could be without poems
lacking strife.

interlude

this is not that kind of poem. in the little
reed hut in the ancient cemetery
we scared some little kids.

At that time we could not have imagined
The sandy shores that would
Be washed away in the torrents of emotion.
                    I paid for my
egg and left the diner,
only to fall in with a real estate agent
and an old woman who at first wouldn't get into the car.

+++

I am quivering with anger

I guess I didn't keep the nightmare of sooth.

I know you are impractical

I watch the mailman put mail into my mailbox
Thankfully. They have identified me as a bibliophile.

I smile and suck my teeth

disgustingly

            like Dracula

+++

The glimmering garnet set in crystal
Vibrated in the universe. The universe was a bowl
Where you could not go up.
Angrily I dashed my child's brains out against a rock

Heartbrokenly
Groping amongst the flowers.

+++

It sounded like the soundtrack to my other life

It sounded like background music

Stretching out into a fourth dimension

She was a great admirer of Henry James.

The card with the heart on it
Was my heart (playfully).

I tell you we will meet again.

it's embarrassing but I haven't read her book. I take her pony by the
halter and lead it around the ring. The people laugh and say how
disarming I am. Despite everything I go on succeeding.

sound of rainwater turning to spaceship asteroid noises
actual sound of a goldfish breathing
Congo drums

The ringleader

Swirls his whip

Attractively and I drink my Grandma's SlimFast.

At nine we go outside and examine a tulip.

At 10:05 we go to the library only to discover it locked.

We go back to her room.

We watch sad Vietnamese movies until my aunt arrives and gives me a hundred dollars.

+++

She is getting angry at me though she doesn't stop. I keep asking you to come home. The school bus pulls away with its myriad kids. The Third World is waiting around the corner and what are we doing? We're trying to put carbon dioxide under the sea! George Bush wants to go to war and there's no stopping him. I retract—am I going back? The plastic cork expands like the styrofoam it is.

My teeth feel like they belong to someone else. I go for a walk around the house. I really ought to enter a time zone but I'm too aerial. I run out of ideas. Tomorrow I want to go to the beach, which has snow on it.

The interiors of my books are all waiting for me. However, unlike the other poets I do not enjoy swinging on vines across the void.

where are you? What shall we have for dinner?

I pant and stamp like a heifer

What DOES God say?

+++

So saying I disappear into the past. My time is up but I keep going off.
White with rage I make presumptuous presuppositions. You laugh at
me because I am murderous like a gull.

Is there anything else I would like to add? Yes, I'd like a vacation to
some beautiful spot in the country, thank you.

Soon I will almost die.

Thirty seconds later I check my e-mail.

If I am going to fly over Britain I might
As well fly over Scotland. Is that right?

The last time I go up I smile, dancing.
The area behind my nose is dead.
It takes a week to repair me.

+++

Squidlike I retreat into my
Underwater lair.

Jesus Christ! Are we having dinner or not?

We scratch each other until we are all bloody.

We talk about early Klee.

Nonchalantly we
brush our teeth.

That's how it ends: with me watching you
As you look at the paintings

+++

This review starts here. Where is everyone? I want to make some
statements about the health of poetry today. Poetry today is unhealthy!
The introduction into my intestine of bacteria
Alarmed me. I was writhing in agony when you approached me,
Napkins stuffed into your ears.

With my death in pain I stalk toward you

This is fabulous, this part. Wait for him to come home
Brought back to the museum.
                                        I cry out

Sarcastically but you are not listening. When will we ever
Perceive one another again?

The sounds around the corner
Hint of discord. Are we going to see you tomorrow
Or eat lentils and rice in the dark?
Writing furiously I curl up in bed,
I can't believe I didn't see what I saw with you,
Circuit-breaker

Where were you? Tired noises

tired ethics
in the driveway

it's the truth
that's wonderful

a magazine subscription

running out

shaking doubtfully
I questioned whether it was true.

I visualized blue rabbit hutches.
The wine was almost black.
Complicated confessions.
When will I see you again?

Lost dignity
"How perfect you are"
not exactly
Supertextual

THE SUPERTEXT

flying cape outstretched
is gone now. It is practically the same
As it was. If my heart could sidle up
To you it would.
I'm not going to work tomorrow.
I'm not going to work until Monday.
Art is not about being nice to people.
The stupidity of afterwards
The beginning of later.

another piece of evidence.
Staring willingly at the sun
While talking about the moon.
You have to admire him
For being wrong   his sister.
Someone to write to in code.

While I look at the moon
The sun grows cold.
Priority is dark
In the slot machine of eyes.
The sack of avocadoes
Stay hard and green,

My heart isn't broken, just sunburned.
In winter we wear a fat coat
I'm ashamed to show you.
Until today
I tried not to believe you
When you said
Kanga would turn against Roo.

Sad tastebuds
Get in my way.
The color of another word
Hides behind an insect
Crawling on the glass.
I wiggle the root of my little toe
And wave my leaves at you.
My desire is summer-colored.

The sand plants
Gather round. I've forgotten about the
sand dollar. I've forgotten the observatorium
Feelings aren't as real now
as they were. Beautiful grass
Hovers below. A rabbit
hops under the house, startling me
out of my dream. I can
hear them screaming in Cairo.
I bury my head in your arms
Before you can snatch them away.

It wasn't there
Where you said I would find it.

It wasn't in the room
with the single houseplant
and it wasn't in the
accidental antechamber.
The funny thing is how the mind
wanders, looking.
I hope I can explain when they find my letters
Though I'll be dead then.
The sun warms the bugs
And I see your shirttail
In their wings. Let's go
somewhere nice, I say
Gesturing at the ocean.

My snot is blue.
Errata snips
Escape from it.
I wish I had a similar organ
For expressing emotion.
The face in the mirror
Is not mine, it isn't even
A face but a footprint
In dogshit. When you signal
To me I come,
Suspecting you of an ulterior motive.
Your face is like a blue olive
Covered with tiny pimples.

+++

The snark is hunted in the dead of night
In a city of triangles.
Overnight my heart
Undergoes a full-service wash
Emerging fresh as a daisy.
Trying to hear through the wad in my head
I see a girl in a red dress.
She is picking flowers and skipping.
When you come home you want to write
And I want to talk. What if I went in
One day for you, one day for me?

I want to write one of those, you know, really good poems
That people always like
But I'm not a good artist,
I don't want to work,
Just sit idly typing to Mozart.
I'll allude to something you feel,
But don't expect me to be capable
Of thought. Children have such nice dreams,
Vague ancient memories of sea and sky.

It may or may not be true
Extraordinary abilities
As you fear.
Lightly skipping on the surface of water.
What happens to the moon in these cases.

I shouldn't have to ask
At the dawn of awakening
The answer like a crumb of suet
at the center of a swarm
of bees melts in the sunlight.

Rejected by Einstein
I swim in humiliation.
I am not the real thing.
My hair doesn't love me.
The answer is clear.
It is like working from brown to black.
Remind me why I'm not special.
Look at me in the dark.

It's what sticks in the form.
My sister looks at me with pity.
She too loves me
Because I have sand.

You will have to adjust
To being a minor poet
He said somberly
Taking my raincoat.
A green light burned on in the attic
While we talked
Without thinking.
So much was going on
Without me.

It is something one deals with
Even as he denies it
The toilet paper leading to the bathroom
The footprints on the red carpet
Leading to the personal assistant.
I didn't see that I was wandering in circles
To avoid walking a straight line.

They are simple codes
They take the edge off
I laugh, the head fog

In the world of smart people
I learned who I was
The evidence was irrefutable
The results were infuriating
I thought I would die tomorrow.
But I didn't die, I lived.
There's a frost for gardeners.

There's the angel of my death.
Eating a popsicle
And smiling. Shredded rabbit
Lies in a puddle in his dish
And the olive oil is fruity.
Let's feel anything but this.
If I see you in St. Louis
Will it be with a floozy?
To avoid being trampled,
Avoid pissing off buffalo.

Hopefully someone will think I'm special
Soon or I may have to go back to my job
As a personal assistant
My best chance is not to die
By throwing myself out a window.
The cobweb blindfold is off;

All I want is to hide.
By then the codes
Were not me
The musicians were not them,
They were not the musicians.
The sad old carnival machine
Beside the dashing coaster.

Sad metaphors

In my image. Sooner or later
You would have learned
You were meant to have children.
A few liked to look at me,
I learned how to feel
In pleasing ways. Knowledge came
With the intimation
That the world was more competitive
On the upper levels.
I wanted to ride with them
But they just looked embarrassed.
Go back to driving a cement truck,
They said. Then there was a
respectful hush. For a day
I hung out at your house.
We looked at a black hole
And took it apart
To see what was inside.
It's been a long time
Since I was a salmon
In a trout stream in Oregon.

I can see in the painting which is also a mirror
A picture of my intellect
With red pins where the thoughts are
And green pins where the emotions are.
The emotional side is off for now
And slowly the red dots
Are disappearing too. Like Monopoly hotels
They are indestructible.

On days when God is nice to me
I turn my face upward to the sun
Like a buttercup.
Don't lie to me, I'm drinking
To your health. One searches for compliments
In the grass of an Easter basket
Which actually used to be real grass.
One finds only letters.
The letters self-destruct too
And as I think about what I want to say
You forget we're in a church.
Even ballerinas lurch
When they dance with the wrong people.

I too am fond of
Seeing the blue sky in the window.
What is there to avoid
Or to be dead of
If that's not the truth?
Flinging himself brokenly about
He was reassured by the
Purple.
All the news comes together
On this dangerous trip
Into the foreseeable future.
In the spare parts room of my brain
I find the missing one
And clothe it in metaphors.
Museums and institutions
Continue to delight and amaze.
When you close your left eye
I see
Purple.

That's when he said patiently
I can take it apart.
There's a light that goes on inside.
There are the stupid aliens
And the smart aliens.

The stupid aliens
Sharpen the knives.

I reach into the hole in the tree
And something bites me on the hand.
Cursing I wipe my hand on my skirt.
The idiocy of smiling occurs to me.
The minutes do not walk—they amble.
That's the answer.
The obverse of the moon is death,
Spiky vision: I poke fondly at the objects
In the box. I retrieve my bottlecap from Geneva,
My yellow winkle from France,
With pursed lips and frowning brow
Obtain the plastic object
From Africa. There is yellow light
In my eyelashes and it's
Too late to make dinner.
Let's outrun the others.

If I could fly to Cairo
With my hand on a stewardess's ass
And my foot on her friend's tits

I would postpone my scholarly duties
Until June. What goes on
In real people's lives is a compromise.
My cat trustingly loves me
Safe from the knowledge
That could not hurt her anyway.
It is better to write
Once a week at the most.
Otherwise we could be heroes
And miners of our own coal.
The stupidity of the green watering can
In the otherwise world

+++

THE EVIDENCE ACCRETED

I read interviews with Borges and a biography of Orson Welles.
I listened to you explain how you built your computer.
You were too nice to tell me
What I didn't want to know. I drove all night
Connecting the dots. I'm going to kick this habit,
I vowed, even as I vaulted into another nightmare.
The colors of the summer house
Were far off now,
I could not get you to talk about your ideas.
It was decided to let them play war
As long as it did not spread
Beyond Iraq. In a hushed voice I begged
You not to drink from the cream pot,
Lovely though it might be.

+++

I walked with my sister
Over lungworts. A bird
That was not an osprey
Endeavored to discern rodents
In the field below.
That is one of those things
You say to people
To make them feel better.

By four I am done with you
And you blow away like a bit of paper
Pissed on by a disagreeable dog.
Look in this room: Here you can see
A woman self-destruct.
Blood leaks out of her ear only to be
collected in a vial.
But it is she who is vile.
It is she who is in white.
It is her in her autobiography.

Alone with cars
Wednesday afternoon.
It's good for me to meet you,
I should stop showing you
My petticoat,
What awakened my frenzy
Was the night flower

Unfolding like the moon
In an opal sky.
With a dead face it greys.
Worlds diminish in intensity
and biota. You point
at me in the mirror and
pretty soon I go out.
My red bra is assisting me
To lift my tits. Everyone has them
But not everyone knows
What to do with them.

In March Mama came to the beach
And walked along the sand.
In June came Papa with his big stick,
His boat, and his net.

The sun and the stars stand for you
From now on. A little curiosity remains
In the cracked teacup, fueling
My hatred of poodles.
When I woke up this morning
I felt like a dishrag without any soap.
Flossing is fun
If you don't do it too often.
Reading your tube of hand cream
I vibrated my rabbit.
That's when I lost my affection
For my nose.
Either one of us are thin.

Many years later I see you on TV
Looking strong and tan.

You have just invented something new.

POEM FOR MATT

It is my magic feather. It flies only at a height of one thousand, two hundred and twenty-three feet. Above or below that it plummets to the ground, or flies out of the solar system.

I try to trick myself into thinking my magic feather goes higher or lower.

Poetry is my magic feather.

. . .

The little tiny flying saucers are dead.
They are pretzels.

Sometimes I wish I were a bird and could fly out of my body.
Sometimes I think of myself thinking this and think, now really.

Today I am getting sucked into my feelings.

Birds are cool.

. . .

EVA HESSE

He made a wooden bird and everyone came and looked at it.
He supervised a series of latex snake-things from his hospital bed.

Because we knew a story about his mother, we appreciated his art even more.
His mother had jumped out a window
Following her escape from Nazi Germany.
As a result there were many windows in his work.
What am I trying to say?
                    EVA HESSE IS A MAN.

Someone is wishing he had a room with four white walls that he could deface
With a pencil, the snow reminds him of paper

WARM LAP GAME!
I am flying along the second level,
And then I am climbing up the inside of an octagonal barn, and I am scared,
And there is ash in the johnnycake I eat on my visit to the eighteenth century
but
At least it's not raining,
The snow makes the house look like candlelight and I find myself
Tossed carelessly in a HAMPER,

Only after she had stepped away
From the easel did he see that she
Had been working on a postage stamp-sized painting of an abstract poem.
That's very nice, he said, May I?
And he put it in a box he had labeled
ARTIFICIAL KNOTTY PINE.

You know how it looks when the snow is blue,
The benefit is ruined,

Later, the snow about to slide off the
Frozen rhododendron leaves
Does,
They consolidated their gains
And now everybody has forgotten them except us

The laughers and the snarlers,
The collaborators and the corporations,
Waiting for the butterfly to land on him like an idiot.

. . .

Nobody is out in this weather, it's snowing and it's getting dark,
you can see me in my window writing, we haven't spent money on
books, that much is clear, and it's obvious that we can't even relax,
having bought the whole line offered to us by disgusting persons
trying to act like they were children of aristocrats. Finally it's too
dark to see anything and I replace the window with the curtain (at
least, that's what it looks like), and try to experience the cells at my
physical extremities, vibrating like undersea corals. I'm ice-skating
on the surface of my brain, which is like a frozen pond, and someone
important is offering me his hand to shake. By staring too hard at the
arm I disturb my chi which starts to circulate rapidly, giving me the
shakes, but luckily I can still laugh and talk about what I used to talk
about.

Oh my, I do like that art.

I do think it's hard to think of poems.

A poetry joke: A Language Poet and a Black Mountain School Poet
and a Fence Poet are sitting around chewing the fat. What do we have
in common? asked the Language Poet. But the Black Mountain School

Poet was tired of stupid poetry jokes. He wanted to go to Asheville and smoke pine needles.

The Fence Poet kept getting up and going to the bathroom. HAHAHAHAHAHAHAHAHAHA!!

. . .

The old poets are afraid
The young poets will find out
They aren't interesting.
The young poets are afraid
Of getting old.
I have been cold all day, said the lemur,
Hatefully.
When will people talk about my poems?

You can't trust me, I can't help being mean and clever. In a lot of the poems I AM JOKING.

People who complain about writing poetry should be ignored. So when I came around the corner of the building and saw those columns of windows with fluttering curtains, you can imagine what I thought. It occurred to me that a funny piece of installation art would be if you got one person to jump out of each of those windows at the same time.

When I die, I want to be a hare on the ground.
Most of all, I want to be like you.
I want to say what I said before, which got me in trouble.
You can't keep a good man down!

I don't know, am I very shy?
Can you write poetry when you're high?

Did you say you saw me in tears?
Did you put your tongue in my ear?
I ought to take my editor out for a coffee/beer.

It was when my brain started showing its teeth to people that I became
LAUGHING MAN. Fluffs and fluffs of poetry were in my hands, it
was like being in a cloud. My hair peeled back and there were the teeth
all exposed in a row like a dog's jaw. Everyone clapped!!!
But it was as if my brain had clamped down on the dog's leash and run
off trailing the happy crowd.
I had never had my brain in my stomach before!!

Just leave me alone with the girl in the casserole, I'm licking her
incredible neck, and get those laughing, tuxedo-clad, mermaid-tailed
lobster claws out of the picture. God damn it,

Let's start over. I need a pair of pants to go with my shirt, I need a pair
of boots to go with my hat, I wish I lived in a factory where you had
everything you needed to make anything you wanted.

Happy, flapping wings
It's easy for me to fly away
From the darling of fools
With my hat-burns
Repeating the stupid game of fuck you

Though I am young, I am as old as she is
And I don't forget, there isn't an
Afterwards to pain

My book is already a classic,
Do you know what that means?
You and I are the United Front.
We are the stupid man's poetry.
All I want is to be happy,
For people to throw
The equivalent of flowers at me.
I might as well speak now, no one will listen later.
I whine on your face. It's a thousand years
Since I dyed my hair green
And wore a macaroni necklace.
How much do you control?
Nothing, people take your stuff

God, it's happening

I'm disappearing
I look like Versailles
And my teeth are clean

It is a question of how large the soul
Can get, when it is afraid,
Can it fill a whole room
Or erupt from a box
As the monkey-fingered mind
Works restlessly at the lock
Of the chest in which a diorama
Is coming to life:

I'm afraid! I say and everyone identifies with me
Little do they know, Bob
Dylan won't answer my letters

. . .

They turned his body brown
No . . . no . . . no . . . no . . .
When you slept in the leaves
Did you ever think
Everyone would
Covet your toothbrush

Is life what you do naturally or what you produce in your struggle
against what comes naturally, i.e. do you resist or give in, it will all be
clear later, do you learn from anything, or is it all something you alone,
frail

No, and like a flower
Exuberantly puking
On the world, I
Laughed, and it wasn't
Beautiful . . .

Is there anything to learn, let us lie side by side
In our Adirondack beds,
Sniffing the beeswax-scented air
Tapping out click-songs

You have a baby and I
Look at it and
Think of screaming
Because I am still a child

Going around museums
And being told not to touch
Getting quite drunk
And smiling, and laughing
As the
Radio
Babbles
On
And those who are dead
Are venerated and those
Who are venerated are,
Surprise, dead,
Poetry is a big cliché
And I want to die.

But I don't, I just want to be left alone
To cry because words aren't as permanent as things

The trouble with poetry
Is it has to come
Out right the first
Time. You can take notes
Toward poetry, but the only fun
Is writing poetry and in pursuit of it
People think they are a genius.
You can never know, it is a long way
From the grass-sleds of your youth,
The in-line skates, it's so easy
You want to throw up,
You're like a man's body
In a spotlight squirming
As if, without hands, to hurt itself
Breaking your teeth on the curb.

Let's be the happiest we've ever been, holding hands, laughing, please
don't
And no,
Won't someone answer my questions,
Poor thing with rolling eyes, so what if it's the last

And anyway, you won't know it . . .
The history of art is boring and shameful
And even the artists are bored and ashamed
And don't have health insurance,

So what's new?

Like a little brown amoeba I swim
Down the bottom of the glass of port.
My sister is there.
We're warm.
Our parents are also there.
They're fighting.
That night I drink so much
I have foggy eyes.
Father, I scream, but I am screaming in my 1980s voice
And he is listening with his 1960s ear.

My father turned sixty-three today.
It wasn't a big deal, but we all noticed.
Life is like—pain.
Don't be stupid, I said—uncompromising.
Don't sell it for fame.
God! The brass ceiling
Fights against obliteration.
Not knowing, anymore—
Never knowing again, never

Able to go back
The words are broken
Beyond repair

The childish park ranger
Extends his arms
Burning, why did you go there
Ticket Booth Man
Skull hospital

In the dark,

Reaching for what isn't there.
Angel who are young
As we were, and yet

Will never be our age

Pity is vile
You, looking at me
In the deserted restaurant
On some cheesy
Bahamian island, can't know
That when I was your age
Everyone hated me, and cast me out
And it really sucked.

Somehow, I know I am making a colossal mistake
But can't prevent it
Life is rushing toward me like snowflakes
In a car and
The lawn is a cushion
I'll tell you what it cost

I'll tell you what it's like
To have your aptitude measured
As I sit in the dark and glare
Into the uncompromising eyes of
The wolf who shops at TJMAXX

Oh God,
It could end there

We were children, and we opened our mouths
And the music played the same as before
The same as for our ancestors
Not knowing how it had gone before
I'll buy anything you say
And die, and fall, and sleep
And fall asleep
Because the only thing to fall back on
Is like dust on the wind
Tropical canary dust
I speak for that fragment, that sliver
That never went to war
But perished anyway

God looks like a bright time
Wishing we had said what we felt
Fighting, and surviving
Life can go by
In the flash of an eye,
And I knew (it's easy to say then)
You ought to have known

Everything would work out,
And make you sick

I'm done after this . . .
Expensive . . . latex dresses
Can you go on, dressing gown
We are so alone
We can hardly hear

They were photographs of men
In a bathroom.
Were they all in the bath at the same time, like in Japan,
Or were they photographed at different times
In the same bath? They look like Jesus,
Classical nudes, Calvin Klein ads, pornography, of course
They make you think.
Or are interesting.
Or pleasing to the eye.
Or shocking.
They make you worry about your elderly parents.
Which of these assertions are false?

. . .

There is a can of juice.
How wonderful it is to read something that is not trying to confuse you.
It makes you feel that person has something to say.
Which is not to say that it is not "difficult."
Do we need a manifesto?

I don't understand how my space heater works, but I'm sure if
someone explained it to me I would find it very interesting.
Who knows anymore. What if nobody likes what pleases you?

There is
A wide range.
Why should I hate my God?

All this time I have been trying to write like someone else.

The rotating pronoun poem.
The parable poem. The "I'm just thinking" poem. The poem-destroying
poem. The "lookit my underwear" poem. The political poem (not very
often). The love poem. The suffering wife poem.

It would be hard to be my husband. I am like a spider with big claws.
If my husband doesn't tell me I look beautiful five times a day I get
depressed and want to kill myself. This is a big problem, because
then he has to stay home from work. My husband works very hard to
support us.

The cat has discovered a way of sneaking around the plants.
Next she will learn to snorkel.

People are reading it and telling other people and in some cases even
buying it for other people.
Secretly, I was happy.
You know what I mean.

FIN

Fence Books is an extension of **FENCE**, a biannual journal of poetry, fiction, art, and criticism that has a mission to redefine the terms of accessibility by publishing challenging writing distinguished by idiosyncrasy and intelligence rather than by allegiance with camps, schools, or cliques. It is part of our press's mission to support writers who might otherwise have difficulty being recognized because their work doesn't answer to either the mainstream or to recognizable modes of experimentation.

The Motherwell Prize (formerly the Alberta Prize) is an annual series that offers publication of a first or second book of poems by a woman, as well as a one thousand dollar cash prize.

Our second prize series is the Fence Modern Poets Series. This contest is open to poets of either gender and at any stage of career, and offers a one thousand dollar cash prize in addition to book publication.

For more information about either prize, visit www.fencebooks.com, or send an SASE to: Fence Books/[Name of Prize], 303 East Eighth Street, #B1, New York, New York, 10009.

For more about **FENCE**, visit www.fencemag.com.

FENCE BOOKS

THE ALBERTA PRIZE

The Cow	Ariana Reines
Practice, Restraint	Laura Sims
A Magic Book	Sasha Steensen
Sky Girl	Rosemary Griggs
The Real Moon of Poetry and Other Poems	Tina Celona
Zirconia	Chelsey Minnis

FENCE MODERN POETS SERIES

Structure of the Embryonic Rat Brain	Christopher Janke, judge Rebecca Wolff
The Stupefying Flashbulbs	Daniel Brenner, judge Rebecca Wolff
Povel	Geraldine Kim, judge Forrest Gander
The Opening Question	Prageeta Sharma, judge Peter Gizzi
Apprehend	Elizabeth Robinson, judge Ann Lauterbach
The Red Bird	Joyelle McSweeney, judge Allen Grossman

FREE CHOICE

Snip Snip!	Tina Brown Celona
Yes, Master	Michael Earl Craig
Swallows	Martin Corless-Smith
Folding Ruler Star	Aaron Kunin
The Commandrine and Other Poems	Joyelle McSweeney
Macular Hole	Catherine Wagner
Nota	Martin Corless-Smith
Father of Noise	Anthony McCann
Can You Relax in My House	Michael Earl Craig
Miss America	Catherine Wagner